MW01278292

The Doctrine
Of Common Good

Itai T. Mupanduki

Trafford
PUBLISHING™

www.trafford.com

North America & international
toll-free: 1 888 232 4444 (USA & Canada)
phone: 250 383 6864 ♦ fax: 250 383 6804
email: info@trafford.com

The United Kingdom & Europe
phone: +44 (0)1865 722 113 ♦ local rate: 0845 230 9601
facsimile: +44 (0)1865 722 868 ♦ email: info.uk@trafford.com

10 9 8 7 6 5 4 3 2

This book is dedicated to those suffering and dying from HIV/AIDS in Africa and elsewhere while the world watches and to those who yearn for a better world yet aren't sure where to start. I hope this book impacts you to act.

Many special thanks to friends and colleagues for critiquing this book and also my special appreciation for the time and effort of my editor Angela Aidoo without whom the book would not have been completed. Special thanks to Rick Yamashiro who illustrated the cover of this book.

CHAPTERS

1

INTRODUCTION

I DO NOT see the contradiction between science and religion in so far as creation is concerned. Who is to say that God did not use evolution to create? Some may say the BIG BANG couldn't possibly have happened from nowhere, but wait a minute, where did God come from? We can never, as frustrating as it is, answer questions about the very beginning. Some have faith and others continue to probe. What I see are humans with intense questions and curiosity about their past, present and future, grappling with death and the desire for immortality. "Surely death cannot be the end," they say. Life is unfair and no two lives are ever the same. Some are born gifted, some are bestowed with wealth from birth, yet others are born into poverty, with disabilities or with illnesses. People then feel that there must be an equalizer somehow, somewhere. Our intelligence, our sense of what is right and wrong is evolving right before our own eyes? Today in every five year period or so, our fund of knowledge doubles due to new scientific and social discoveries and innovations. No more is slavery acceptable. Human trafficking is now a crime, and people continue to learn more about human rights and better governance. Global interaction between different races is the highest ever. Racism, though still existing, is now an embarrassment for many. We are beginning to appreciate the repercussions of human activity on the environment. And the list goes on and on.

Once in a while a person with exceptional capabilities is born, bringing with them new ideas that radically alter our path. People such as Buddha, Socrates, Jesus Christ, Karl Marx, Mohammed, Gandhi, Einstein, Ford, Kwame Nkrumah, and Martin Luther King to name a few. Yet, these people as they live on earth are still mere mortals. We still must collectively decide what to do with the information they impart.

The economist Karl Marx would stir in his grave if he found out how profound his book changed the course of history, by creating the Soviet empire, mighty China, the cold war, divided nations like Germany, China, Korea, and Yugoslavia, not to mention smaller revolutions all over the Southern Hemisphere.

Einstein gave the world a chance to harness energy to produce electricity and bring development to all four corners of the globe. Some self empowered sons and daughters of man, instead abused this opportunity and decided to create weapons of mass destruction. This responsible collective decision making process needs to be rethought so that we may not continue to blunder. It is the poor judgment of some of the sons and daughters of man that now has us with all the know-how, resources and knowledgeable people, yet the world is still grappling with poverty, hunger, wars, persistent human degradation, greed, disease and illness, terrorism, racism, gender bias and the list goes on. The world is divided between the rich and the poor. Some spend billions going to space, while others desperately need just a few millions to escape from hunger and poverty. Some make millions from essential medicines, while others die daily of largely preventable diseases. Such is the fate of humanity.

It would seem that in the current scheme of things, this select human irrationality of some is so pervasive and unshakable to the point of humans in general giving up on their future and believing in an unavoidable doom, Armageddon or ultimate meltdown. Yet, I say there is also a universal truth that humankind needs a daily struggle in order to survive, that this daily struggle can be misdirected to self destructive acts, that this energy for the daily struggle can also be redirected for purposes of good. This is not at all a new message, for ancient wisdom states that "a lazy mind is the devil's workshop". Put in another way, this is the factory of irrationality. Another universal truth, in my opinion, is that we are brought up and shaped by our past and our environment to live within certain shells. Thus, some grow up to be Atheists, Christians, Moslems, Hindi, Taoists, Democrats, Republicans, Communists, Right wingers, Liberals, members of the developed nations, citizens of poor nations, and so on. It can be very hard, if not impossible to break open these shells and see another person's point of view, especially when one is bound in their own shell. The challenge for mankind becomes, how to gather enough energy and momentum to break from these shells and let the yolk and albumin from the eggs within flow and mingle and come up spontaneously with one progressive accommodating shell."

Some big minds in the past have hinted that the world needs a new social order. A great idea indeed but the question is, "What kind of social order?" The sons and daughters of man, since ancient times, rarely agree on one thing. They have different ideologies and political minds, different religions, different social classes and different levels of development. The hunger for power, ambition and greed often militate against the common good. It becomes easier to preserve our shells, live in them and maintain the status quo. As we all know, wealth seekers can never be nation builders, let alone humanity builders. It is very good to make money but the real sin is dying with the money. As I alluded to earlier, it is my firm belief that from time to time people are born with exceptional abilities to create wealth. The problem arises when these exceptional talents are then used against common good, and money becomes a weapon to extract more and more from the ordinary person. This is a problem to be tackled by responsible collective thinkers, bearing in mind that those who can make money should be allowed to make money and use it well. I believe that when the sons and daughters of man read these words, they will be quick to say "this is an infringement on intellectual and personal property, this is big brother watching, this is communism revisited, this is another form of tax to create yet bigger government, this is a disincentive for anyone to work, this is a threat to inheritance laws already overburdened with government demands and so on and so forth"

The shells are tough to break indeed, but I would like to ask "What kind of social order do you envisage for your great grandkids, knowing the way things are going today?" For, if we do not tackle these issues properly, then what we think is terrorism, what we think is disorder, and what we think is poverty, will pale in comparison to what is to come. I am not a prophet of doom. On the contrary, I have great hope in our future, which is why I write this book. This hope comes from the fact that most of us are rational beings. Deep inside, we are all deeply troubled when a fellow human being is ill or dying. We sympathize when there is a tsunami, earthquake, hurricane, or famine in other parts of the world. Why? Maybe because God lives in all of us, and each and every one of us is an image of God. Maybe because we appreciate calamity and accept that there is strength in numbers. Who would want to be the sole survivor on earth? Therefore with this premise, it is possible, given adequate information, for the sons and daughters of man to marshal the willpower to do what is right for the future of mankind. To break from their shells and let the yolk and albumin mix freely and spontaneously grow.

Many have stood at many pulpits and preached change without prescriptions. Thus some will ask if I have a prescription. My answer is simple. The task is so daunting that it requires many minds. I will also say this, I may not know the path, but I sure have seen where it should lead. And this is no Utopia because as I said earlier, today humankind has all the means to address most of our problems. I will now explain in detail where I think we should be going.

2

Borders

FIRST AND FOREMOST, as it was in the beginning, we must abolish all borders as we know them today. Yes, abolish the borders! Some will immediately jump and say their countries will be flooded with immigrants. Governments will say they do not want to facilitate a brain drain, in the name of sovereignty. Others will say they do not want their countries to be turned into developing countries. Others will say they have no desire to facilitate the spread of terrorism and radicalism by opening wide their borders. Others will say they cannot open their doors to religious fanatics who have caused mayhem in many other places. I say to you, yes you are right, those things may happen. But I would also ask you to think about it further. If all people can truly move freely and all those in positions of authority know this, if we so much fear poverty and underdevelopment, then what other better incentive do we need to channel resources into human upliftment than this very fear? That fear is the tool that will switch off unrealistic military budgets and force us to start building roads and highways, irrigation networks and factories, schools and universities, hotels and hospitals wherever they are needed. This will encourage the true free flow of technology and information. That can only spur further growth and development and wealth for all concerned.

As it is we live in a very segmented and segregated world with little fiefdoms here and clubs of the wealthy there and envious poor nations across over there. The rich are getting richer and further milking the poor. The poor are getting poorer and trying to escape poverty by any means possible. The middle class is fast disappearing everywhere. Huge multinational corporations are getting more powerful than most governments. They will continue to get stronger and eventually even displace governments. These corporations are not nation builders but profiteers. The current situation is not sustainable, and as I alluded to earlier, will lead to chaos. How many small governments have already been overthrown for bananas, bauxite, diamonds, oil, land and other resources? Those who think military force can be a substitute for social and international justice are dreaming. The human being historically has had immeasurable resilience in fighting oppression and injustice. If we refuse to learn from history, then none but ourselves will be to blame and surely our great grandchildren will curse us.

Each day that passes and we delay implementing that moral justice, we are in effect denying justice and laying the foundation for revolt and chaos. Everyone can see the signs, but we allow ourselves to be misled by people with dubious agendas who *could not* care less what happened to anyone else, as long as they profited and their dogs of war guarantee them some temporary safety. Is it not true that some of the so called terrorists have genuine political and social claims? Is it not true that one group of people in their own shell label some terrorists, or insurgents, or saboteurs, yet another group will view the same people as freedom fighters, liberators, or the only way for the voiceless? Is it not true that so called democracies can tolerate tyrannies and ignore oppressed nations in the name of free markets and oil or diamonds? Is it not true that so called progressive nations have trampled upon the aspirations of smaller nations and groups of people? Have we not seen the stalemates on political and economic issues, and on matters *whose solutions* were perhaps obvious but *for strategic reasons or corporate profits became very difficult to resolve?*

As we all know we now live in the information age. The world has shrunk and become a very small place. Atomic bombs can now be carried in suitcases. Chemical and biological weapons are easily transported. Radical human elements prey on the abused, weak and suffering. A hungry man is an angry man. A peasant does not have much to loose but a hoe. We therefore need to act now.

How do we work towards abolishing borders? Again this is not a task for any one person, but for all of us. We must begin to realistically and collectively look at these issues.

3

DEMILITARIZATION

SECONDLY, WEAPONS OF mass destruction must be eradicated completely. No nation has the right to have these weapons of mass genocide. *As long as one nation has them, other nations* will feel threatened. No nation has moral authority over *the rest of humankind* and the right to have such weaponry capable of destroying earth a thousand times over. The real issue here is that some nations harbor ambitions to control the whole world for their own benefit. *That* sort of thinking, in the long run, is very detrimental and self defeating. The money spent in *the* senseless cold war *alone could* have transformed the world into a much better place. We do not need another such era. Yet what are we seeing? Even more deadly weapons are being developed and there is talk about war in space. *That* is crazy!

The root cause of militarization historically has always been the need to control world resources and expand hegemony, not self defense as some would want us to believe. Thus, tied to the eradication of borders is sovereign demilitarization. We do not need various global armies to foment trouble. Train a soldier and he or she must at some point try their new weaponry or want to have a *taste of* battle.

The nations of the world must have one global military to tackle issues like terrorism *and to* assist in global disasters. With time the *military* as we know it must completely change to serve more as a developmental agent, by performing such duties such as protecting huge factories and installations from rogues.

It is also not sufficient to eradicate these weapons of mass destruction and allow the proliferation of small and light arms. The flow of small arms must be curbed and eventually stopped, in so far as this is central to prevention of deadly conflicts. A time will come when these weapons will be mere sporting goods like swordsman ship and javelining today if we work hard on this issue

4

LAW AND ORDER

THIRDLY, A GLOBAL police force focusing on law and order -fighting drug trafficking and whatever new vices come with human progress- will guarantee individual safety and enforce the global laws. It is a fact that humans will always be faced with good and bad, but as we eliminate poverty and hunger, I do believe that being rational beings, the crimes will become less as everyone will be guaranteed a job somewhere on earth. As it is, Interpol, the International Criminal Police Organization, exists with about 186 member countries and already plays *a* role in fighting terrorism, organized crime, illicit drug production, money laundering, weapons smuggling and child pornography. However, it has to remain politically neutral and can not venture into racial, military, political, religious crimes which are today the biggest threat to global peace and progress.

While the cold war is dead, a new religious divide between the Judeo-Christian and the Moslem-Sharia camps continues to grow, fueled by mistrust and greed for power and money, and historically rooted in the right wing Judeo-Christian crusade and the fanatical Islamic Jihad. On the surface it would seem, if one only listens to political rhetoric, that the Moslem- Sharia camp wants to spread Islam across the world, and that the Judeo-Christian axis, led by USA and UK, wants to spread democracy across the globe. But look more closely. The Moslem world knows clearly that the Anglo-American politico-economic institutions are too powerful and will not succumb. They also know that realistically it is not feasible to convert these nations fully to Islam. The Anglo-American governments on the other hand, despite what they say to their populations, are quite aware that the Moslem brotherhood and even Al Qaeda are opposed to what they see as economic plunder, exploitation, tyranny *as well as the* sustenance of unpopular but definitely strong regimes in Egypt, Saudi Arabia, Yemen, Jordan, Israel, who *are not democratic by* any measure, in the name of preserving economic interests. They also know that these regimes are made stronger through support from Europe and America. *These Islamic* groups now see the promotion of Sharia law as the most if not the only economically just way to distribute the wealth in the region.

Clearly the most logical way to diffuse tension would be to guarantee truly popular governments in these countries, who would in any case still sell their oil to Europe and America. *However, it* seems common sense is not that common and for now the common man or woman shall be told, until they go deaf, about clashing cultures, about the threat of Islam or the threat of Christianity or Judaism. On their part, failing to overthrow these largely unpopular regimes in the Middle East the Al Qaeda's and the Moslem Brotherhoods, and many such other groups shall continue to foment trouble and chaos in the Euro-American axis. *This new* religious divide, at least in the eyes of the common man, will continue to fuel itself to potential Armageddon.

We have a World Court or International Court of Justice (ICJ) established *as far back as* 1945. *The ICJ sits* in The Hague, *and its main* function is to settle international legal disputes submitted by member states. We also have an International Criminal Court *(ICC)* established in 2002 as a permanent tribunal prosecuting for genocide, crimes against humanity, war crimes, and the crime of aggression. Their mandates are also limited, but the idea is noble. For example, the UN Security Council is to enforce decisions if a member fails to comply with rulings of these courts, but the same Security Council has five veto wielding members which essentially means a decision against any of these five members is hard to enforce.

I will site two examples. In 1966 and 1968 the UN Security Council imposed mandatory economic sanctions on the illegal Smith regime in Rhodesia. However by 1969 Nixon and Kissinger who only saw Africa in the east- versus west perspective typical of the cold war era, and were keen to curb perceived Soviet advances adopted the so called "Tar Baby Option" which meant supporting the few remaining white minority regimes in Southern Africa including Rhodesia. Thus in 1971, in direct violation of international law the Byrd Amendmend was passed which essentially permitted the US to import chrome and other minerals from Rhodesia. Secondly in it's relentless efforts to overthrow the Sandinistas in Nicaragua the US again violated international law and in 1986 decided to withdrew from compulsory jurisdiction by the ICJ rather than deal with this "veto wielder versus ICJ" issue after the court ruled in favor of Nicaragua in" Nicaragua versus the USA" in 1984.

Only member governments and not individual entities (for example huge multinational corporations, *which are now often* bigger and more influential than most small governments, and can break international law while also breaking their own national laws) *are subject to the jurisdiction of* the ICJ. Recently in the USA we have seen US Congressional inquisitions into the activities of companies like Halliburton *which* have blatantly defrauded the tax *payer* in America, while also engaging in unfair trade practices in occupied Iraq and the Middle East. Thus while the USA can convict for tax *payer* crimes, it is quite clear that it would not push too far in prosecuting it's own in international issues which would backfire on the USA.

On the other hand the International Criminal Court so far *has only about* 104 *member* countries while *another* forty one countries have signed but not ratified the statute. *The USA, China, India* and a few other states oppose *the ICC treaty. The Court's* mandate currently excludes terrorism, which was found difficult to define to everyone's satisfaction, drug trafficking and the use of weapons of mass destruction. Also there is no means to ensure that countries do not pass *contrary* laws as happened with the US *Congress'* passage of the American Service Members Protection Act (ASPA) which denies aid to many of the poorer countries that ratified the *treaty* establishing the ICC, as well as creating bilateral immunity agreements preventing individual states from surrendering Americans to the *ICC*.

If we could agree on a basic code of laws especially encompassing *the* elimination of weapons of mass destruction, terrorism, oppression, fair international *trade*, acceptable laws governing separation of religion and state, laws promoting cultural promotion while allowing universal standards of education, demarcation of global electoral zones, modes of promoting a universally acceptable means of governance and policing: then be able to create a powerful police force to enforce these laws under the auspices of one grand international court system, then we would have *transformed international* law and order, on a global *scale* and also empowered a global judicial system. *The global* judicial system can then be allowed to develop into a powerful third wing of the global governance promoting checks and balances on the global executive branch and representative branch as they also evolve and prevent the inherent limitations and contradictions between the ICJ, ICC and the Security Council and powerful individual member states we see today.

Thus anyone creating *illegal* arms, developing weapons of mass destruction *or* fueling conflict in any form must face the wrath of global law enforcement and trial by the international courts. No part of the world should be exempt from this rigorous policing, enforcement and punishment if the rules are *violated*. In today's world we have a weakened International Court of Justice where some nations are non signatories yet when convenient will advocate for use of the court.

The world witnessed genocide in South Africa under the Apartheid regime, which was a member of the *UN; in Tibet where China,* a veto wielding member imposes its will and continues to displace people, in Vietnam and Cambodia where millions died under American bombs; in Chechnya where Russia, *another veto wielding member of the Security Council,* continues to suppress the wishes for independence and self determination *long* after the end of the cold war; in Rwanda where *nearly* a million preventable deaths occurred while the Security Council remained hesitant. *Also, in* Angola where *cold war politics* and the politics of oil and diamonds caused much suffering and many deaths, in *the former* Yugoslavian territories where the race card and religion were allowed to play leading most notably to the preventable Srebrenica massacre and many other chilling massacres, and *most recently* in Lebanon and Northern Israel where we saw the Security Council paralyzed to inactivity due to the veto wielding power of the USA while *many* died and property was destroyed, as Israel and *Hezbollah* fought, in Iraq where the whole international community stands helplessly as the only superpower oversees mass murder, displacement of Iraqis and an increased efflux of refugees to other countries, all in the name of regime change, elimination of non-existent weapons of mass destruction and of course oil. *Further* in Sudan where the proponents of an Islamic state under Sharia Law wantonly massacre and displaces people while the government is protected by China's veto, to name a few. *Yet,* sadly where a semblance of justice occurs only the small nations and the *powerless* are held accountable.

We were told Pol Pot was the problem in Cambodia, *Milosevic* in Former Yugoslavia, a few leaders were prosecuted in Rwanda and so on, yet those who war-mongered, supplied the arms, fueled apartheid, financed and benefited from the conflicts in one way or another, the power brokers or economic powerhouses behind these conflicts largely went unnoticed *and unpunished. In fact some of these guilty nations* were part of those who advocated only for the punishment of the smaller power brokers.

In Korea, Vietnam, Cambodia, Zimbabwe, Angola to name a few, the scourge of landmines and their silent *homicidal* and crippling crusade continues unabated yet it has been impossible for the world nations to agree on a moratorium or ban production of these weapons conclusively. *That is because* some simply refused to sign or ratify these agreements. The USA remains one of the largest producers, exporters and collectors of landmines and will not sign a treaty banning these weapons. In fact *the US* is developing a newer *and* more advanced form of landmine. China, Russia, India, Pakistan, The Koreas, Cuba, Turkey, Myanmar, have also not signed the treaty. China, Russia, the USA, Pakistan, India Poland hold in stockpiles the largest number of antipersonnel mines. In future, those making, marketing, stockpiling, or using such dangerous arms must face the full wrath of international law and also be made to pay damages to the individuals so injured. It should be very clear to anyone that any time a weapon is created, the intent is obviously *harmful.* It should be amply clear that the ultimate solution is *the* eradication of these kinds of weaponry and technologies for as long as some *nations have* them, others will be tempted to *possess them as well.*

My dream is clearly a world with a one truly functional *global* police and judicial system operating *freely.* Only then can we say we are in a new era *because* eras are defined by fundamental changes in the institutions governing society.

5

CURRENCY

FOURTHLY THE WORLD only needs one currency. Economic textbooks go on at length telling us about the *benefits of the monetary system. What those books omit* is that in today's world there is good money (also called hard currency), and bad money, not acceptable for international transactions. I say everybody needs good money and in fact only one kind of money for that matter, for the true virtues of money, so clearly described in books of economics, to be attained by all. This will guarantee free flow of wealth, unrestrained global investment and also do away with trade barriers since there will be *no need for protectionist trade policies.* We will create a formidable global middle class. In essence a lot of the problems we have today arise from *the wealthy* wanting *even* more and not giving economic space to others. One *global* currency allows unrestricted human innovation, productivity and *unrestricted* markets for everyone and anyone who can produce. It also creates consumption opportunities for everyone.

With free movement of people, one currency and one military *as well as* one global police force, the path towards a true representative world democracy and government are not hard to imagine, *and* why not? I do believe that a new kind of governance will naturally emerge, a system *of government* that will be global in nature with locally relevant representation. And who knows, maybe in the distant future humans will actually solve most of their problems and not even need any form of government at all.

Now that *is* Utopian, but what a world that would be for our great grandchildren. They will then look back and say

"You know, what they called the space age was actually the dark ages and what they called the information age was actually the age of enlightenment"

So as we search for peace, unity, tolerance, non violence, understanding and overall, human progress lets all make this the era of enlightenment.

6

GOVERNANCE

WHEN PRESSURE DROPS it can conquer dread: *(necessity breeds invention)*. Global warming, international terrorism, AIDS *and* SARS have clearly proved that when threatened, humans have an enormous capacity to cooperate, and tackle global issues and let global consensus prevail. Based on *that* premise therefore, and using currently existing institutions *(*no matter how flawed*)*, I believe that a core group of thinkers could look at this issue and find ways to influence public opinion. For me the journey clearly started with writing this book. I do hope that global citizens will read *and critique it*, but also grasp the fundamental *underlying* message. We have huge problems with this task but they are surmountable.

Already we have in existence, the United Nations, a global organization that was founded on sound principles. If you will permit, I would like to refer you to the Universal Declaration of Human Rights which I will quote verbatim. It reads:

Universal Declaration of Human Rights

(OTHER LANGUAGE VERSIONS)

Adopted and proclaimed by General Assembly resolution 217 A (III) of 10 December 1948

On December 10, 1948 the General Assembly of the United Nations adopted and proclaimed the Universal Declaration of

Human Rights the full text of which appears in the following pages. Following this historic act the Assembly called upon all Member countries to publicize the text of the Declaration and "to cause it to be disseminated, displayed, read and expounded principally in schools and other educational institutions, without distinction based on the political status of countries or territories."

PREAMBLE

Whereas recognition of the inherent dignity and of the equal and inalienable rights of all members of the human family is the foundation of freedom, justice and peace in the world,

Whereas disregard and contempt for human rights have resulted in barbarous acts which have outraged the conscience of mankind, and the advent of a world in which human beings shall enjoy freedom of speech and belief and freedom from fear and want has been proclaimed as the highest aspiration of the common people,

Whereas it is essential, if man is not to be compelled to have recourse, as a last resort, to rebellion against tyranny and oppression, that human rights should be protected by the rule of law,

Whereas it is essential to promote the development of friendly relations between nations,

Whereas the peoples of the United Nations have in the Charter reaffirmed their faith in fundamental human rights, in the dignity and worth of the human person and in the equal rights of men and women and have determined to promote social progress and better standards of life in larger freedom,

Whereas Member States have pledged themselves to achieve, in co-operation with the United Nations, the promotion of universal respect for and observance of human rights and fundamental freedoms,

Whereas a common understanding of these rights and freedoms is of the greatest importance for the full realization of this pledge,

Now, Therefore THE GENERAL ASSEMBLY proclaims THIS UNIVERSAL DECLARATION OF HUMAN RIGHTS as a common standard of achievement for all peoples and all nations, to the end that every individual and every organ of society, keeping this Declaration constantly in mind, shall strive by teaching and education to promote respect for these rights and freedoms and by progressive measures, national and international, to secure their universal and effective recognition and observance, both among the peoples of Member States themselves and among the peoples of territories under their jurisdiction.

Article 1.

All human beings are born free and equal in dignity and rights. They are endowed with reason and conscience and should act towards one another in a spirit of brotherhood.

Article 2.

Everyone is entitled to all the rights and freedoms set forth in this Declaration, without distinction of any kind, such as race, colour, sex, language, religion, political or other opinion, national or social origin, property, birth or other status. Furthermore, no distinction shall be made on the basis of the political, jurisdictional or international status of the country or territory to which a person belongs, whether it be independent, trust, non-self-governing or under any other limitation of sovereignty.

Article 3.

Everyone has the right to life, liberty and security of person.

Article 4.

No one shall be held in slavery or servitude; slavery and the slave trade shall be prohibited in all their forms.

Article 5.

No one shall be subjected to torture or to cruel, inhuman or degrading treatment or punishment.

Article 6.

Everyone has the right to recognition everywhere as a person before the law.

Article 7.

All are equal before the law and are entitled without any discrimination to equal protection of the law. All are entitled to equal protection against any discrimination in violation of this Declaration and against any incitement to such discrimination.

Article 8.

Everyone has the right to an effective remedy by the competent national tribunals for acts violating the fundamental rights granted him by the constitution or by law.

Article 9.

No one shall be subjected to arbitrary arrest, detention or exile.

Article 10.

Everyone is entitled in full equality to a fair and public hearing by an independent and impartial tribunal, in the determination of his rights and obligations and of any criminal charge against him.

Article 11.

(1) Everyone charged with a penal offence has the right to be presumed innocent until proved guilty according to law in a public trial at which he has had all the guarantees necessary for his defence.

(2) No one shall be held guilty of any penal offence on account of any act or omission which did not constitute a penal offence, under national or international law, at the time when it was committed. Nor shall a heavier penalty be imposed than the one that was applicable at the time the penal offence was committed.

Article 12.

No one shall be subjected to arbitrary interference with his privacy, family, home or correspondence, nor to attacks upon his honour and reputation. Everyone has the right to the protection of the law against such interference or attacks.

Article 13.

(1) Everyone has the right to freedom of movement and residence within the borders of each state.

(2) Everyone has the right to leave any country, including his own,

and to return to his country.

Article 14.

(1) Everyone has the right to seek and to enjoy in other countries asylum from persecution.

(2) This right may not be invoked in the case of prosecutions genuinely arising from non-political crimes or from acts contrary to the purposes and principles of the United Nations.

Article 15.

(1) Everyone has the right to a nationality.

(2) No one shall be arbitrarily deprived of his nationality nor denied the right to change his nationality.

Article 16.

(1) Men and women of full age, without any limitation due to race, nationality or religion, have the right to marry and to found a family. They are entitled to equal rights as to marriage, during marriage and at its dissolution.

(2) Marriage shall be entered into only with the free and full consent of the intending spouses.

(3) The family is the natural and fundamental group unit of society and is entitled to protection by society and the State.

Article 17.

(1) Everyone has the right to own property alone as well as in association with others.

(2) No one shall be arbitrarily deprived of his property.

Article 18.

Everyone has the right to freedom of thought, conscience and religion; this right includes freedom to change his religion or belief, and freedom, either alone or in community with others and in public or private, to manifest his religion or belief in teaching, practice, worship and observance.

Article 19.

Everyone has the right to freedom of opinion and expression; this right includes freedom to hold opinions without interference and to seek, receive and impart information and ideas through any media and regardless of frontiers.

Article 20.

(1) Everyone has the right to freedom of peaceful assembly and association.

(2) No one may be compelled to belong to an association.

Article 21.

(1) Everyone has the right to take part in the government of his country, directly or through freely chosen representatives.

(2) Everyone has the right of equal access to public service in his country.

(3) The will of the people shall be the basis of the authority of government; this will shall be expressed in periodic and genuine elections which shall be by universal and equal suffrage and shall be held by secret vote or by equivalent free voting procedures.

Article 22.

Everyone, as a member of society, has the right to social security and is entitled to realization, through national effort and international co-operation and in accordance with the organization and resources of each State, of the economic, social and cultural rights indispensable for his dignity and the free development of his personality.

Article 23.

(1) Everyone has the right to work, to free choice of employment, to just and favourable conditions of work and to protection against unemployment.

(2) Everyone, without any discrimination, has the right to equal pay for equal work.

(3) Everyone who works has the right to just and favourable remuneration ensuring for himself and his family an existence worthy of human dignity, and supplemented, if necessary, by other means of social protection.

(4) Everyone has the right to form and to join trade unions for the protection of his interests.

Article 24.

Everyone has the right to rest and leisure, including reasonable limitation of working hours and periodic holidays with pay.

Article 25.

(1) Everyone has the right to a standard of living adequate for the health and well-being of himself and of his family, including food, clothing, housing and medical care and necessary social services, and the right to security in the event of unemployment, sickness, disability, widowhood, old age or other lack of livelihood in circumstances beyond his control.

(2) Motherhood and childhood are entitled to special care and assistance. All children, whether born in or out of wedlock, shall enjoy the same social protection.

Article 26.

(1) Everyone has the right to education. Education shall be free, at least in the elementary and fundamental stages. Elementary education shall be compulsory. Technical and professional education shall be made generally available and higher education shall be equally accessible to all on the basis of merit.

(2) Education shall be directed to the full development of the human personality and to the strengthening of respect for human rights and fundamental freedoms. It shall promote understanding, tolerance and friendship among all nations, racial or religious groups, and shall further the activities of the United Nations for the maintenance of peace.

(3) Parents have a prior right to choose the kind of education that shall be given to their children.

Article 27.

(1) Everyone has the right freely to participate in the cultural life of the community, to enjoy the arts and to share in scientific advancement and its benefits.

(2) Everyone has the right to the protection of the moral and material interests resulting from any scientific, literary or artistic production of which he is the author.

Article 28.

Everyone is entitled to a social and international order in which the rights and freedoms set forth in this Declaration can be fully realized.

Article 29.

(1) Everyone has duties to the community in which alone the free and full development of his personality is possible.

(2) In the exercise of his rights and freedoms, everyone shall be subject only to such limitations as are determined by law solely for the

purpose of securing due recognition and respect for the rights and freedoms of others and of meeting the just requirements of morality, public order and the general welfare in a democratic society.

(3) These rights and freedoms may in no case be exercised contrary to the purposes and principles of the United Nations.

Article 30.

> Nothing in this Declaration may be interpreted as implying for any State, group or person any right to engage in any activity or to perform any act aimed at the destruction of any of the rights and freedoms set forth herein.

While I think that in future the terms "individual nations or countries" must be replaced with "regions of the Global Government", the wording of the document clearly illustrates and already advocates for "The Doctrine of Common Good". Clearly this *Declaration* was born out of noble goals by visionary and noble men and women but unfortunately at the same time was created and has remained governed in a flawed manner reminiscent of the post Second World War era when the Allied Forces emerged victorious. Though meant to be a democratic institution, the United Nations remains largely undemocratic and mired in the Cold War era and its divisive political and economic alliances.

First it has the undemocratic Security Council comprising the five giants of the cold war People's Republic of China, France, Russia, The United Kingdom and The United States, all with veto powers, then everyone else. Before smaller nations can push through any agenda, they have to align with one of these power brokers to avoid vetoes.

Also today with only one superpower left, the agenda of multilateralism is slowly sliding and the UN is loosing credibility real fast. The permanent members on their part are not likely to easily relinquish their positions of privilege and advantage in the current world order. The organization is under-funded and lacks political muscle.

The United *Nations (UN)* is also very reactive to most issues instead of being proactive. The *UN*, though well intentioned, finds itself compromised by the above issues. A good starting point would be recreating the United Nations to reflect *circumstances in the world today, and* take it from there. The Security Council as it stands is now an anachronism and must be scrapped and replaced with a fairer system. The *League* of Nations, as some may recall, was dissolved for having failed to prevent *WWII*. If the United Nations does not measure *up* to current problems and as an organization evolve sufficiently to meet contemporary challenges, then no-one should be surprised if it meets the same fate *as the League of Nations*, a verdict which, in my opinion is *far* overdue as we all review the *Declaration of Human Rights* and realize that the doctrine of common good was more than implied in 1945, but that we as humankind have largely steered off the course.

Net worth and military might should not be the main considerations in garnering power in a democratic institution. The voices of the people need to be heard and listened to. I sincerely believe in one man one vote and I do not see why all the nations preaching democracy, equal rights and rule of law become so hypocritical when it comes to an institution of such significance, a catalytic powerhouse for global change if allowed to stick to *its* founding principles and become truly democratic.

Population based representation today would seem probably the fairest when it comes to voting at the United Nations and elsewhere in line with the principle of one man one vote though as it is it violates the *sovereignty* of nations, which *many are* currently *unhappy with* anyway. Similarly, for now financial contributions *to the UN* must continue to be based on *member nations'* Gross National incomes as well as per capita incomes and contributions from those entities *which* can *make contributions*, but *the* capacity to contribute has to be divorced from voting capacity.

Periodic calls for reform have characterized the United Nations, but the various meetings and sessions have largely failed to hit the nail on the head. *That is* because of the inherent contradiction of the veto power. Perhaps a final breakthrough on *that* issue will eventually come. Perhaps the current lone superpower's unilateralism will galvanize nations and other groups to rethink issues. *That* may turn out to be a good starting point towards creating a more democratic

United Nations. *The* organization can then *be further* improved upon and transformed into the global authority on policing, militarization, currency reforms and freedom of movement as outlined above while remaining truly representative.

The challenge we now face is that the world is caught up in *its* own mess. Having created a problematic global structure in the first place, it is very hard to sit down objectively and introspectively and reform *these structures from within.* National interests will always stand in the way of global progress *or wealth* seekers will always block the way. Power brokers will not want to loose control. *However,* having said that the fate of our future and of generations to come depends on us acting today, on us doing the right thing, on us recognizing that if there is mayhem we can all perish and destroy the very things that we all cherish: *the peace* and that is peace, prosperity, understanding, continued human upliftment and fraternity where everyone looks out genuinely for the other.

However I still say I have a lot of faith in humanity and this can still be accomplished. It will take time but it is doable. If events in global environmental issues can be taken as a barometer of global opinion making, then one can clearly see that we can bring positive change to our decision weak, bureaucratic, and *anachronistic* United Nations. *Let's* either use this existing structure efficiently, constantly reevaluating our progress towards a better future or scrap it, having learnt our lessons and start anew.

How then do we deal with the inherent bureaucracy of government as we know it, especially if we are to create one trying to cater for the whole, diverse world with *its* numerous religions, political views and multitudes of cultures and languages. Again I think we can use already existing structures with some modifications. I applaud Europe for trying to create a functional common government and economy and a unified currency though: I dislike *their* protectionist tendencies and arm twisting of the poorer and weaker developing nations.

The United States of America is another very good example of what unity of diverse people and states can bring in terms of prosperity for *its* people even though the country itself still has huge problems in terms of special interests and lobbying groups hijacking democracy.

Economic inequalities largely persist, racial discrimination has been *difficult to eradicate* despite legislation; and there are inefficiencies in resource utilization to wipe out disease, ignorance, human degradation or forge global peace for that matter. It is said Americans will always try everything else before finally embarking on the right thing. The problem today is that America is the global leader economically and militarily and when it sneezes the whole world may just catch a cold.

History has also shown us that where political and economic priorities are misplaced, *and* justice is denied, *political* amalgamations can easily fragment. We saw the British *E*mpire and the Soviet empire collapse. Hitler and the Nazis showed us that unity can not be achieved through force and war mongering and human degradation. These are unique blue prints and case studies whose positive lessons can be adopted in many regions. We must learn from history.

Even where unions already exist, more and more countries can be further co-opted and integrated as equal partners until eventually a human Gondwanaland *is reconstituted.* It is clear the Universe has no center or edge. It should also be evident that the earth is a globe and should function as such interactively for humans. We already have a world with some little fiefdoms calling themselves countries. I believe in *self-determination,* but I also believe in *the* efficient use of human and material resources. Twenty tiny neighboring countries, each having a government, a civil service, diplomatic service, heads of states, parliaments etc is a waste of resources and if all of these countries could democratically merge they could become more efficient and improve the welfare of their people. *That is,* assuming they evolved into more efficient governance which I know is ultimately *necessary* as humanity's endless needs and scarce means will always clash. I believe if regions work cooperatively we can with time end up with no more than five countries world wide. *That* would be a stepping stone towards a truly unified representative Gondwanaland government geared towards global prosperity with no human left behind enjoying the economies of interaction.

Of course current *para-national* unions have been created largely as protectionist economic and political entities. *That* sort of thinking however would have to be replaced by the doctrine of common good as we gradually work towards a diverse but unified system that still allows self determination through *the ballot box. The difference will be that we will* now use all our resources for continued collective prosperity, peace, unity, tolerance, nonviolence and better global understanding.

Who is willing to relinquish political and economic power in these amalgamations? As I said, we need a new way of thinking, a new doctrine of common good *as well as* a true belief in representative democracy. The current United Nations was founded on the inviolability of *the sovereignty of* nation states. But the cold war saw the creation of proxy nations without much *control over their sovereignty. The* post cold war era has seen the only superpower violate this very tenet by for example invading and occupying Iraq under the false pretense of eliminating weapons of mass destruction which the *same* super powers and their proxies possess.

We have seen a powerless International Atomic Energy Commission used to further the agendas of the super power while remaining silent on confronting Nuclear proliferation sanctioned by the super power in Israel, India and Pakistan. Despite the lessons of the second world war we are beginning to see the gradual remilitarization of Japan, again sanctioned by the only superpower in *its* search for allies in its invasion of Iraq. Did we not see all this before with Hitler, Italy and Japan? The effects of global insecurity today, the fueling of a silent regional arms race, the displacement of people, the violent takeover of a country have *all* gone by without a single cry for enforcement of international justice against the perpetrators. *That could be* for fear of retribution, but I say mainly because the United Nations has been rendered impotent. Its role is considered obsolete by the very *superpowers*, the USA and Britain instrumental in its formation in San Francisco in 1945 and they are probably right, but for the wrong reasons.

Further, during the Iraq war, the so called Geneva Convention in treating prisoners of war was quietly discarded when a new *class of prisoner:* "enemy combatants", was created by the Bush administration as the world watched helplessly intimidated by the "You are with us or against us" doctrine. These *enemy combatants* were then clandestinely taken to CIA bases all over the world including Guantanamo. We also saw *heinous* crimes at Abu Ghraib prison, the likes of which can only be addressed by a new International Criminal Court *to which all nation states are subject.*

That was followed by the fastest trial and execution of a former leader in modern times *while his country was* under an occupying force and a puppet powerless government. *When* Saddam was, to put it mildly, hanged for "crimes against humanity" while the perpetrators arguably were *committing* the same crimes against humanity as evidenced by the desire to have the Abu Ghraib prison *razed* to the ground rather than be preserved as the Auschwitz of tomorrow. The American military would subsequently try their own for crimes committed against Iraqis, who were not *allowed the* supposed due process *available to the Americans.* In Afghanistan, families of innocent victims murdered by the occupying military were given a *paltry* $2000.00 as compensation and the matter was laid to rest. I was left soul searching as I remembered the billions Libya had to pay for the similar *heinous* terrorist murders of innocent westerners killed in *the Lockerbie* plane bombing, yet in *that* case the compensation was *determined by a western court* and considered fair due process. *In the case of the victims of western violence in Afghanistan,* the families had absolutely no other recourse under a puppet Karzai government. Justice delayed is justice denied and history will live to record these wrongs and double standards.

Also America's refusal to ratify the ICC and its creation of unilateral agreements with poor aid hungry nations to protect it's military from international prosecution should leave some, if not caution many, about its long term intentions as a lone superpower that refuses any form of restraint. But erasing the site of Abu Ghraib will not erase the event, the injustice, the greed for oil, it will not bring back the innocent thousands murdered since the occupation nor will it mend the mistrust so created.

Clearly a new entity with new provisions has to emerge from the current UN. But first and foremost, the world needs to reestablish confidence in international diplomacy. *As a start,* all nations must be equally accountable and punishable: then we can forge forward. Also for starters International agreements, once ratified by a two thirds majority of nations, should in my opinion, be considered universally binding. With this there would not be non-signatories to globally binding treaties to important institutions like the International Court of Justice, the International Criminal Court or The International Atomic Energy Commission. With responsibility must be attached accountability on a global scale.

We need a system where the man or woman with the best agenda for common good runs for office competitively. The era of nationalism should be fast disappearing as we work towards true global integration as outlined above. Regional leaders should truly be architects of progressive global policies.

Mass education of global communities must be a priority. I have always wondered why an organization of such importance as the *U*nited *N*ations does not have international radio and television stations, newspapers and websites to articulate its goals above and beyond what individual nations do.

For many in developing nations, the United *N*ations is seen in moments of crisis when one of its wings appears as peace keepers or drought relief agencies or when government officials attend or return from a UN meeting in New York or Geneva and local newspapers cover *such events. Other occasions include* the case of the US when an unpopular leader like Fidel Castro or Hugo Chavez uses the podium against the US or when a US leader rallies the UN for support for example the misinformed Colin Powell justifying attacking Iraq . Having had the privilege to live in the United States I was astounded by how little the general public appreciated the role of a truly functional United Nations, rather ironic for a nation housing the very general assembly of this organization. In most cases views about the United Nations were dictated by the local media. Thus in seeking a global mandate to go to war in Iraq for example the mass media reported the importance of garnering support through the UN. However when this failed and the "Coalition of the Willing" was formed there followed a scathing attack *on* the UN as a corrupt organization embroiled in a corrupt oil for food program in Iraq. In all this the true role of the

United Nations was never articulated. As we work towards a unitary system I think a powerful global mass media campaign on public education can not be ignored.

Electoral campaigns must be viewed as screening tools for those with the best policy ideas to lead. *Time spent in elected office* should be a time to activate these formulated policies to better global human existence. We need a system without special interest groups hijacking government.

Indeed there is hope. Those following global events will recall the recent stalemates at the WTO global conferences and the subsequent emergence of the groups of 20, 30 and 90 to counter the G8 and its Breton Woods institutions as well as promote South-South Cooperation. It is such activities and actions which clearly demonstrate the un-sustainability of the present situation and also show the true aspirations of the majority of mankind while laying bare the preposterous greed of a powerful few.

It is ancient wisdom that all it takes for evil to succeed is for good men and women to do nothing. As more and more resistance builds, the powerful will eventually capitulate, though not without putting up a fight, and we will see the emergence of progressive leadership. This ultimately becomes a win-win situation for everyone because as long as the people are happy with that caliber of progressive leadership, then that leadership will have the office and *be able to sustain the momentum of progress*. At the same time public *service* will have to be assumed as a responsibility and not a privilege, it will need complete accountability and no patronage.

Today the paradigm of dualism dominates i.e. black and white, good and bad, rich and poor, North and South and so on. But, as I said earlier, we live on a globe. How many dimensions does the globe *have*? 360? 3600? 36000? *Who* knows? They are infinite. *The world should also have infinite dimensions*. A multidimensional projection of humanity and its desires and aspirations, but like a globe spinning in the same direction on the same axis and maintaining a consistent day and night yet allowing regional variability in its topography as humanity matches toward unparallel progress: *it is* all before us.

What languages will be used? Again the United Nations where

Arabic spoken as an official language in about twenty four countries or so, Chinese spoken in two countries by about 20% of the world population, English spoken officially in about fifty two countries, French officially spoken in twenty nine countries, Russian spoken in four or so countries officially and Spanish spoken in twenty countries officially, Canada with an Anglo-Francophone coexistent culture, India where major languages are used separately in religion, politics and a democratic multilingual federation, Ethiopia which has maintained Geez as the religious language and Amharic as the official language, Tanzania which was instrumental in promoting Swahili and The European union where they are teaching their citizens to speak more than one commonwealth language, have shown us the way. Language is an integral part of human culture and must be promoted and respected. Language is also a unique heritage for a people and therefore must be preserved.

Having said that, history shows us that throughout human development in various communities some languages have been the main medium for commerce and politics, other languages have been unique in religion, yet many other languages have been passed on from generation to generation, undergoing a vibrant transformation with human development. Other languages also went extinct or near extinct. People need to be encouraged to learn to speak more languages to enjoy our human heritage. Interpreters will always remain indispensable especially in global political and economic discourse.

I have been personally impressed by how some Asians can use the same basic sign alphabet to read in Chinese, Korean, Japanese and other languages. I think we have something to learn from *that*. Thus, *for example,* everybody can understand the sign for rice or fish but can only say it in their own language. Trade and commerce can thrive easily with such a common tool of communication in this era of rapid communication tools. The only down side *will be having to learn* the six thousand or so Chinese alphabet characters, *that can be done*. We already have all the tools we need, we just have to harness them.

As more people share languages a natural bond emerges, and as more and more people mix and mingle, understanding, tolerance and human developments are further fostered.

How will the *global* government operate? In my opinion a decentralized federal system- like government with regional governments and a main United Nations like central location is elected, but in a more democratic and diversity inclusive way. Again these institutions have to be viewed as constantly evolving and adapting to human needs guided by the doctrine of common good and human preservation. Global electoral zones will be demarcated and regional and Global representatives appointed accordingly. With the technology at our disposal and new innovations to come people will even be able to vote from their personal computers in their own homes as technologies become fairly distributed across the globe.

Will multinational corporations disappear? As much as we are all witness to the destruction of natural habitats, defiling of culturally sacred sites, degradation of forests wild life and fisheries, commercialization of traditional festivals, forced relocation of aboriginal peoples (stretching from the San in the Kalahari for diamonds, the Masai in East Africa for pyrethrum, tea and cotton, the Bayaka in Central Africa Republic for logging, the Amazon Indian for logging and farm estates, the Aborigine in Australia for residential and farm land and so on and so forth all) in the name of profit, and the attendant loss of nutritional, economic, social, cultural, and environmental interests of all. In as much as the powerful nations have funded some of these big corporations by bypassing the United Nations through the International Monetary Fund, The World Bank. The World Trade Organization, or their own tax dollars while all the time milking the poor and powerless dry, I still do not think they necessarily need to disappear. What needs to disappear are *the* practices of corporate greed and malpractice, like we saw *when* the ENRON saga unfolded in the USA, underpaying workers, avoiding taxes and paying dividends, unhealthy work environments, using under trained or improperly trained work forces resulting in ghastly hazards, or not fully meeting contractual obligations as in the case of Halliburton in Iraq (where the US government awarded contracts but found itself overcharged, double billed or delivered with inferior equipment while at the same time profit margins were growing for Halliburton). What needs to disappear are corporate practices failing to adopt environmentally friendly practices and technologies, failing to eliminate toxic and hazardous work environments and not ensuring the good for all. The extensive clearing of forests in South America to make way for mono-crops like genetically modified soybeans that are then chemically fertilized, all to satisfy the corporate greed for bio-fuels is an example of such self-destructive profitable tendencies.

Instead there should be fair and equitable wages and such evil practices like outsourcing of jobs, services and people to cut costs, that are decimating the middle class as we know it today, or forever condemning other nations to inferior wage structures contrary to the international bill of rights, will die a natural death. Child labor which has fueled profits in many poor nations will seize.

The current International Labor Organization ought to be transformed into a global entity with authority to ensure that tied to every job is a transferable pension plan, retraining programs, disability insurance and also availability of a basic universal health insurance for every worker. *That will replace the* limited current mandate for seeking humane working conditions. Clearly there is a lot of room for subjective standards based on what *any* one employer, group of employers or society may consider humane. To make my point clear one only has to look at the variances in work week, benefits, and remuneration between say USA, France and Japan, all three industrialized nations, but rooted in very different work ethic and cultural roots.

Also, since current globalization trends have clearly failed to meet the aspirations of the vast majority of mankind today with regards to provision of decent jobs, decent livelihoods, fair and equal compensation as outlined earlier, the Global Organization's role and framework need rethinking again in line with my earlier proposals. Demand and supply *together with* government regulation should all determine competitive safe industrial expansion. Monopolistic tendencies must face stiff penalties to allow the best products and prices for the consumer across the globe. Special interests groups and lobbyists should not meddle with politics. Also the generality of the public should have equal access to purchasing shares and having other investment opportunities so they become part and parcel of wealth creation.

In this context too the way the institutions like the Breton Woods and the WTO are run needs a complete overhaul to be in line with genuine global development and not serve the interests of a privileged few. It is also my view that *such supra-national groups* need to be centralized squarely under one global umbrella, transparent and accountable to all peoples. Since its inception, the World Bank has always been led by an American largely approved by the US president and then endorsed by the World Bank Board. *Similarly*, the IMF has also always been led by a European. Is it any wonder then, that these organizations today have been largely used by the so called Group of Eight (G8) to bypass the United Nations with its so viewed populist World Council, and that they both serve these economic agendas largely misnamed as globalization, when in fact it should rightly be called G8-tisation.

Growing connectivity, productive capacity, easy transport are not sufficient for globalization in so far as they become tools to serve a few nations to advance their profit motive under the guise of free trade, corporate profitability while actually and ultimately advancing insubordination of true global development to the hegemony of the so called ideology of the G-8.

Underpinning true Globalization must be the advancement of communication, transportation, productive capacity, trade, corporate equal pace with the eradication of the current democratic deficits where human rights, as regards the right of every human to a decent job and livelihood, based on the resources and ingenuity at our disposal, have been trampled upon. *That trampling has been done* largely by the wealthy and self-*professed* democracies whose financial and economic considerations, though in the long run myopic and *not conducive* to international peace and stability, have always overridden the social agenda. I therefore *cannot* see any true globalization at the moment.

As I said I do see further entrenchment of G-8tisation unless and until we start to rethink these things. If we don't the consequences are clear and I shudder to think how many more 9-11s the world would want to endure, how many more genocides, toppled governments, insurrections, and increasing chaos before humans realize the age old wisdom of prevention being always better.

As I said earlier we have the institutions already. They only need revamping, reorientation and sometimes just fine tuning. In the World Bank and the IMF, I see the beginnings of a global central bank and the *creation* of a single currency. In the WTO I see finally the fair regulation and policing of international trade and the disciplining and streamlining of wayward corporations. I *have* already elaborated on the ILO. The Global department of agriculture and food safety is rudimentary in the Food and Agricultural Organization. I say rudimentary because there is a lot of work lying ahead in trying to find the most efficient means and places to produce the most of a particular food while ensuring universal food security and access. Today some nations produce food surpluses which sometimes are damped in the sea to maintain *product* prices, while at the same time, *other* nations, cash strapped by the requirements for so called hard currency, which to me in itself is a tool for underdevelopment, are not able to grow technology intensive foods or have the capacity to import food and therefore end up facing starvation year after year. The current FAO, though tasked with global food security has no other instruments outside the current sovereign nation formula to enforce true efficient food security.

In fact, what we have seen is the creation of yet another agency, the World Food Program, that has not solved the real underlying problem, but rather runs around with a begging bowl in times of crisis further entrenching these hard currency strapped countries in dependency. These are very sensitive matters and as I recall Tolbert's government in Liberia was toppled because the people did not have enough rice to eat. Knowledge and technology must be equitably disseminated. The healthiest food production methods have to be promoted. Human capacity also has to be efficiently developed and assured of fair compensation through a uniform currency formula as I already elaborated.

It is no coincidence that with the demise of the colonial structures and independence of the former colonies where most of the gold and silver came from, the gold standard was quietly abandoned under various new economic theories and models. We all can clearly see who would have been at an advantage if gold had continued to be the store of value. In many ways it was closer to a unitary currency than the current alternative of good and bad money.

A huge task indeed lies ahead but organs of the current United Nations like The United Nations Development Program can be transformed into powerful, well funded global entities to spearhead manpower planning, economic restructuring, resource capacity building, infrastructural development and new technological development and integration on a massive global scale with a unified budget and currency under a global central bank. The outcomes can be astounding and limitless.

In the end the current thinking in the G-8 and Multi-national corporations will succumb to environmentally, culturally, economically, socially and politically acceptable modes of operating and actually become part of the catalyst of change. *Why?* They already have the tools and the know-how, it's only their energy and motive that will have to be redirected. There are many unhappy and disenfranchised constituencies in these same G-8 countries as well where the same widening gap between the rich and poor, the same lack of health insurance, disability insurance, pension plans, homelessness, unemployment, and other forms of social injustice are bound to trigger predictable violent upheavals. *That* was seen in France in 2005 when the youths went on rampage for equitable jobs and equal opportunities.

The power of the vote should be allowed to weed out corrupt politicians who might otherwise meddle with big corporations or create poor socioeconomic policies. All businesses must observe a code of conduct in line with genuine profit making. There is absolutely nothing wrong with making as much *profit as* one can as long as it's made legally, fairly and without denigrating your fellow humans. To give an illustration, in today's world a factory worker in a car manufacturing company in USA earns say US$15.00 per hour, while a similar worker in a similar plant belonging to the same car manufacturer but based in Indonesia will be paid US$2.00 for the same amount of work and with even less benefits. The same goes for the gold miner in an African country today compared to a miner in Germany.

In a fair world economy with one currency and one central controlling banking system and free movement of labor and capital, then all the factory workers may initially want to move to the USA and all the car makers to Indonesia. The gold miners will prefer to work in Germany, while the multinationals will want to mine in Africa as it is today. The difference however will be that because there is free movement of labor and capital with a common currency and universal fair regulation, then jobs and production facilities will have to find equilibrium within *the* legal framework based on universal human rights which will now clearly articulate and stipulate equal job benefits. There will be nowhere to run to except make wages and benefits good for everyone to maximize production and genuine profits.

People in every locality will then think more globally while genuinely acting locally and creating an *unprecedented* network meeting socio political needs and economic development as well as the much desired true democracy, equal rights and good governance. That is the true essence of productivity and the perfect joy in prosperity for all. That is The Doctrine of Common Good achieved.

Can the world religions find common ground? Today most religions have been hijacked by a minority who now dictate what everyone must follow or do due to the power of the purse. Some *of those minorities* have even become strong political powerhouses, for example the Christian conservatives in America. Others have become governments themselves, further pushing their agendas, for example in Indonesia and Saudi Arabia. In both scenarios the definition of Christianity or Islam assumes a political dimension. Religion is now being used as a means to an end, political power. *The result is increasing* religious and political intolerance, *warmongering* and individual, group or state terrorism. The state machinery under *its* various guises is now used to further this religious agenda by these *religious* hijackers.

It is always informative to go back in history to a time when after the Romans destroyed the Jewish state, Christians, Jews, Moslems, *Hindus*, Buddhists, Taoists coexisted in peace across much of the *present* Middle east and Persia. It is also informative to observe that after *the fall of* Napoleon in Europe, the rise of the secular state would follow and that in the USA the religious extremism of some denominations and consequent loss of life led the founding fathers *of the United States* to propose the separation of church and state. In the Middle East itself secular states were also created in Iraq, Egypt, Turkey, Syria. In the far East *as well,* many secular states have existed where different religions co-existed with perhaps India being the best example followed by the Koreas and Japan. Most of these countries have remained tolerant to many different religions growing in their midst.

In contrast, countries *such as* the old India broke up into the *present day* Pakistan, Bangladesh, Ceylon and possibly Kashmir. *The* former Yugoslavia divided between religious and ethnic lines; Nigeria is polarized between the North where the powerful Emir of Sokoto has a strong following from the Northern Islamic parts, and the south which is largely Christian or traditional in *its* beliefs. *Then there is* Sudan, where the North is strongly Islamic and Arabic and the South and Darfur region are largely non Moslem and Bantu; Northern Ireland divided between the Catholics and the Protestants, to name a few. *The regions mentioned* have been torn apart in religious *strife* which has spilt *over* into the political arena because of the various religious elements in government. It is difficult to live in Saudi Arabia and Indonesia *if you are not a Muslim.* Today the right wingers in America view Arabs *resident in the US* as outright terrorists, partly because of the influence of the Jewish Zionists in America and partly because of *the* imposed conservative Christian agenda. Based on the *forgoing,* it is my view that the world should strive for an elected form of government whose structure is completely separate from religious doctrines.

The Universal Declaration of Human Rights document has come under attack as evidenced by the elaboration of the Islamic Declaration of Human Rights (CDHRI) adopted in Cairo in 1990 by the 19th conference of Foreign Ministers of forty five member states of the Organization of the Islamic Conference *(OIC). The CDHRI* establishes the Sharia Law as the only source of reference for the protection of human rights in Islamic countries, yet we are striving to create a global community tolerant to many views based on one Universal Human Rights creed. The CDHRI fails the universality test by imposing *a condition.* Human rights based only and exclusively on Sharia, thus *excluding* non-Muslims. Secondly *the CDHRI* assumes unquestionable divine supremacy over political and legal issues, *a position* which defeats the very purpose of universality. What then if every religious group came up with its own Universal religion specific declaration of Human rights based solely on their divine revelation?

In my opinion therefore, based on the above description, the *complete* separation of religion and state is perhaps the best way to safeguard *the* freedom of worship, religious tolerance and also avoid political strife masked under hidden religious agendas. It is difficult if not impossible to achieve intercultural consensus if political decisions become solely based on religious beliefs. *For* even *within* groups of *the* same faiths, e.g. different Moslem sects or different Christian denominations, *a*greement is rare on many issues pertaining to not only governance, but also basic belief tenets, let alone basic human rights.

What sort of Educational System should the world have? There already exists acceptable international educational benchmarks, *such as* a seven year primary school, four to five year high school, college and university education, with a few differences here and there. There are also *no- traditional* modes of education, *such as* home-schooling, *which* still *follow* the same outlined benchmarks. Then there are the purely religious schools as seen in some Jewish, Islamic, Mormon, Buddhist, Taoist schools. In my view the global constitution must embody individual freedoms and strike a balance between parental, societal and governmental responsibility in so far as the education of the child and individual citizen are concerned. Basic to these must be the freedom of choice and the freedom of religion. Having said that, I still think that the separation of religion and state is also paramount to safeguard individual freedoms. *Government*s worldwide *have* to guarantee an internationally recognized educational standard and benchmarks. Religious studies in schools must replace bible study, Koran study, Tao study, Buddhism study etc. The student should be exposed to religious knowledge across the globe as a purely academic exercise. *That* will, *in my view,* improve religious tolerance as people will have a better understanding of the foundations of *other* faiths.

Separate from the routine government school however, private schools, not dependent on the tax-payer may exist to teach their followers whatever religion they want as long as they also stick to internationally recognized academic benchmarks. People should have the freedom to choose between private and public schools and be guaranteed that at the end of the day the final product is academically the same though there may be religious and philosophical differences. *That* to me should underlie the global policy *of* education for all citizens of the world from birth to death.

Appropriate retraining programs should be readily available to *suit* ever changing work environments and new technologies. Standardization of basic benchmarks in Math, Science, Geography are easier to achieve on a global level while curriculums in language, history and religion will always have regional biases. Many schools of thought abound in economics and all need to be explored to give students a more global perspective as I believe all have positives and negatives to offer.

The thorny issues that need to be addressed include equal gender access to education, technology transfer in disseminating knowledge and research, high level skills training and transfer across the globe, sustainable human talent growth and development with regards to available resources and desired skills and unforeseen needed talents. The global educational system must be robust and efficient in so far as dissemination of appropriate skill levels and flexibility in retraining for any unforeseen skills requirements *are* concerned. Only then can we envisage full employment on a global scale and of course *maximum* productivity.

As development advances across all human frontiers the human factor should never be found wanting. With all the technological innovations of today all that's left is the human will.

What sort of Health care delivery system should the world adopt? We know the creation and evolution and sometimes collapse of institutions in whatever form is perhaps the primary topic of history. While many poor nations have achieved impressive levels of literacy in their populations though they then have to deal with the subsequent and inevitable brain drain in the current economic order, clearly the same cannot be said about health delivery. There clearly is a relationship between economic development and progress in health *delivery*. *That* is mainly because most of the killers of mankind before age sixty five are largely preventable and with good sanitation, good housing, good water and reticulation systems, dust prevention, immunization campaigns, eradication of pests and parasites, public health education in general using all available tools more than seventy percent of illness and death can be wiped out.

Thus health improvement becomes an integral part of overall development. Indeed, even where preventable diseases have been tamed, emerging chronic diseases are only getting to be understood better with newer and better technologies and research capabilities. The human genetic map is being unraveled opening new frontiers in our comprehension of genetic disorders. Yet technology and money are not sufficient as evidenced by the USA, the most affluent nation, spending the highest amount per capita on health, yet more than sixty nine million of its people remain uninsured or underinsured and can not access adequate health care. The age old problem remains the tug between assuring access for all, affordability and cost.

An all inclusive, progressive health care policy is required locally and globally guaranteeing every human being provision of preventive and curative health care, as well as provision of adequate housing as this is directly tied to one's wellbeing. and indeed borrowing on all facets of human development and progress to have a physically, mentally, spiritually healthy being.

> Basic to this policy is making provision of health care a basic human right. That should be followed by the implementation of a global health provision plan funded by taxpayers. In line with individual freedoms, anyone desiring additional private healthcare can acquire a private health insurance policy. This in a way solves the problem of equity, quality and cost, because universal health coverage realistically guarantees access. For those with extra money to spare, additional private insurance will buy them the extra high quality and care they may desire, without depriving the average citizen of essential health care. In other words, the state shall always strive to provide what everybody needs as op-

posed to what everybody wants in order to balance the budget.

As I *wrote* earlier, we do have today all the required resources, but we are *misusing those resources.* Nobody seems to question the wisdom of spending one hundred and forty billion dollars on a war in Iraq annually, when millions are dying of HIV/AIDS, malaria, diarrhea and dysentery, malnutrition, complications of diabetes etc. We spend billions in space exploration looking for life out there when we cannot adequately cater for the current inhabitants of mother earth. What then if we come across an aggressive alien species and they follow us home and find the bulk of earth so underdeveloped and *wallowing* in poverty? Traditional wisdom tells me that charity begins at home but alas. There is no satisfactory Global Health Policy, period.

Once in a while there is an outbreak of Ebola, SARS, Dengue fever or some other rare disease. Fancy epidemiologists globe trot and academic papers are published, the World Health Organization marshals its resources: but once the threat is over, we return to complacency. A global campaign wiped out smallpox yet the virus still is allowed to exist in some so called special labs God knows for what progressive agenda. We are seeing the reemergence of polio due to human complacency and misallocation of resources. The medicines for HIV are available yet not readily affordable as big and powerful drug corporations put profits ahead of human life.

Sadly after a public outcry, we saw a concession made where in the case of an epidemic, intellectual property rights can be overridden and other countries can manufacture these medicines. I say sadly because who is to determine that for their country so many deaths *constitute an* epidemic? I say one death of any citizen of the human race is epidemic enough to warrant action to *provide* medicines. That is why we need universal health care: that is why the whole concept of intellectual property must be revisited when dealing with precious human lives. What sort of creatures have we become that money has become more precious than the sanctity of *life?* Do we not know that a dead human being has become extinct, with their unique attributes and whatever contributions they might have *made* for the earth? Shall the world continue to loose precious lives because they are largely from poor and weak African nations whose leaders signed *on to* the WTO treaty without reading the fine print or without knowing what they now know about AIDS? The deeply entrenched racist attitude of people in Europe towards Africa, *as well as* the "not in my back-yard" attitude of America *do* not help the situation. I am often amazed by how many in Europe and North America care more for wild animals, the environment and their pets than they *do* about Africans. Their governments' attitudes that Africa should be forever a source of raw materials and nothing else do not help the situation.

The wealthy nations quietly create programs for their own populations then advocate simplistic HIV control protocols for the poor. This is the real genocide of this century and a true human oriented international court of justice should be dragging drug corporations and governments to court for allowing this genocide to continue. Those who celebrate space conquest must understand the real price tag.

Yesterday it was the USA and British governments that were reluctant to jump on the band-wagon to end apartheid in South Africa which ensured poor health standards amongst many other discriminatory issues for its largely black population, due to economic and cold war considerations. *Today* it is China in Sudan propping up a murderous regime *that is* wiping out its citizens in Darfur, all in the name of oil.

Again in a fair global system all these countries and their supporters would have been dragged to a true global court of justice and made to pay heavily. As it turned out, the black people of South Africa had to be content with a truth and reconciliation process, while those who propped up apartheid were conveniently forgotten and the Americans and the British became the champions for Mandela and freedom and the band played on. *Today,* many still die in South Africa of largely preventable diseases. As for Sudan we await to see who can challenge a veto wielding China in the UN or how the politics of oil will ultimately play out especially as the Americans become more and more war weary in Iraq and the hidden un-drilled oil in Darfur comes to the forefront of politics.

The inseparability of health policy *and* political economy cannot be overemphasized. Global economic development will spur health*care* improvement. *However,* to guarantee basics a new global health policy will have to be formulated under one umbrella and having decentralized operations. *Taxpayer* guided universal heath coverage with a supplemental second tier private health insurance is proposed to guarantee individual freedoms while sustaining equity in health. The health care delivery institution, in so far as it increases chances of human survival and continued procreation and survival of the human species in my opinion is a very unique institution requiring uttermost adherence to the Universal Declaration of Human rights.

How will smaller industries thrive in a globally permissive and competitive environment? The premise of a new sustainable global system is fair pricing and one currency. Today Ghana sells its gold for say $ US 400.00 an ounce and everyone then buys a gold necklace in New York with that same amount of gold for say $US2.000.00. The cost of making the necklace is probably say $US100.00. Profit realized by the jeweler is more than $US1 400.00. Today Starbucks sells a cup of Rwandese coffee for about $US4.00 in Hawaii. A woman working in Rwanda on a coffee plantation makes $US0.60 per day and Rwanda gets $US60.00 per ton of coffee when Starbucks buys it. The cost of roasting and grinding the coffee are negligible. Here in lies the crux of the matter. With one currency Ghana will obviously develop jewelry factories of its own and Rwanda will process its own coffee. *Actually,* Rwandese will be better placed to market their coffee already ground and packaged to a global market since there will be a unitary currency. In fact Starbucks will not be able to compete that efficiently against the Rwandese companies now selling coffee to the consumer all over the world. Without currency conversions, a lot of middle men will be wiped out and the true producers of a product will become the beneficiaries. Alternatively Ghana will insist on at least $US 1 200.00 per ounce for its gold knowing the final price of a necklace with an ounce of gold.

With this fair trade will ultimately result. As it is, the presence of a few international currencies fairly convertible between themselves and termed hard currencies but holding all other weak unconvertible currencies at bay further promotes exploitation and maintains the status quo and in fact makes technology transfer very difficult. As I looked at this further it became clear to me that if the proponents of division of labor were right, then we should have seen the emergence of three groups of countries i.e. the producers of raw materials, the producers of technology and the manufacturing nations all separate and efficient, but this has not happened, why, because the producers of technology are the same people with the dominant currencies and therefore have ensured that manufacturers are retained within their environments. But this is in conflict with true division of labor as evidenced by unsustainable costs of production in these countries and shrinking profit margins now leading to outsourcing of production. Actually in my opinion outsourcing confirms the need for the existence of an independent manufacturing entity in a separate location.

The thing masking *that necessity* is the existence of multiple currencies, most of which are subjugated to a few. Rwanda today produces coffee and competes with many other coffee producers, not really for global demand (as I will illustrate) but rather for demand as defined by ability to pay in these few hard currencies. Thus Zambia may have the demand in its currency for coffee but Rwanda, blackmailed by the few operational hard currencies would rather lower its price and sell to those who will pay in these few currencies. This not only reduces, true demand, as the demand in Zambia goes unmet, but also impoverishes Rwanda and fosters underdevelopment. *Some* have advocated barter trade but I say *that avoids* the real issue *by* advocating short term solutions in an era clearly defined by the virtues of good money. So let good money and only good money for everyone prevail.

Therefore, in order to unleash unrestricted productive capacity, to realize true global demand, I advocate one simple currency for the whole world centralized under the new global government and run under a *reconstituted* World Bank and International Monetary Fund.

In fact let me use one example, the US car industry. At the beginning of the last century Ford designed the first car and predicted that by the turn of that century every American would be able to afford *a* car. Now to a large *extent,* at this time Americans mined for their minerals, produced their own steel and developed their production lines as different entities in different states. The common factor here was one currency. Everyone, in the production of raw materials, machinery and the auto car thrived *so that* by the turn of the century almost every American in the commonwealth of states using the same currency could afford a car. Of course with time foreign imports were required, for example chrome, largely responsible for the US companies busting sanctions in post UDI Rhodesia and Apartheid South Africa as I alluded to earlier when I touched briefly on the Byrd amendment but my original argument still remains. Needless to say the question then arises as to *how* the small companies can survive when competing with huge multinational*s*? Again I would like to revisit Rwanda. Today many factories in Rwanda can not operate efficiently because they lack foreign currency, coffee growing is labor intensive because of inability to import tractors due to scarce foreign currency or hard currency. A talented engineer in Japan would like to work in Swaziland but won't be able to because the salaries are not competitive compared to Japan, *while* Swaziland cannot be expected to pay that much in scarce foreign currency.

So the question becomes*: why* are nations holding themselves hostage to multiple retrogressive currencies? When an Emperor in China created the first paper money around 7000BC, he had no idea that there would ever be a different currency designed, yet even China has had three operational currencies in Hong-Kong, Taiwan and the mainland. This is madness. People have been tricked and need to come out of their shells. Now, to answer the question I will go back to the most thriving economic giant, the USA. The foundations of the American economy in the past and today remain rooted in the small family business. Many of these then grew into huge corporations and shareholding entities with corporate governance structures. Others like Ford or Kellogg's became huge multinationals. Thus given the same conducive environment, one currency, huge demand, free flow of capital, labor and technology, it is my belief that from all four corners of the globe many family businesses will emerge and grow. The coffee farmer in Rwanda will form a cooperative venture with fellow farmers and process their coffee locally, fetching them better prices. An entrepreneur in Rwanda will market the Rwanda brand in the current Zambia, The Congo and *beyond*. An international business partner will find new coffee markets in Bulgaria and Norway and so on and so forth after all we are talking about a period where information exchange is revolutionary and we have entered true globalization.

I see new environmentally friendly industries emerging and exploitative Multi-national *corporations* collapsing as they *simply won't* be able to thrive in that new legal and progressive atmosphere unless they *adapt.* No longer will it be possible to remove governments for demanding an increase in the price of bananas, no longer will miners work for a pittance knowing the true price of minerals and having an opportunity to be stockholders.

It is at that point that true and phenomenal human achievements will begin to be seen. I do believe strongly that humans have the capacity to overcome their current greed and insensitivity and will create a wonderful global village. I am not one to wait till divine intervention for I believe that in each one of us lives the divine and that collective effort brings everlasting rewards.

How will all this really start? I would like to think that we have already started. We have heard the murmurs from the Southern hemisphere, we have heard the discomfort with the latest unilateral actions of the USA. We have seen *unprecedented* riots in France, we are seeing blood being shed in Israel and Palestine, Chechnya *and* Sudan. We have seen *unparalleled* terrorist actions in New York, Madrid, Nairobi, Jakarta *and* London. The root causes are clear to us; the solutions nevertheless are not so easy. *Yet,* in each and every rational one of us, for what can I say about the irrational, there is a yearning for peace, fairness, human progress and understanding.

It was great minds that formed The United Nations and other peace loving organizations we have today. It is great minds galvanizing people to resist unfair trade practices within even the WTO framework, *it* is great and forward thinking minds that continue to fight against racial discrimination *and to* fight for gender equality.

All these actions collectively gather momentum and like the proverbial Chinese water flowing down the mountain, changing shape but not form and essence till it becomes an immense unstoppable ocean. Every *article* is part of the process. One of these days some nations will gather enough courage at the United Nations to start the formal path towards genuine globalization. Or some civic group will pressure the powers that be. Or maybe another preventable catastrophe will finally jolt our conscience. Then the water will slowly gather more and more momentum as it flows down the mountain. I cannot say with absolute certainty how it will finally really happen.

Is there no danger of cultural hegemony? Human economic development without concurrent cultural, moral, spiritual and physical development cannot be said to be complete. Self determination by local communities in selecting leadership should to some extend guarantee preservation of progressive culture.

Who is to say what is progressive? In my opinion any cultural activity fostering unity of purpose, human dignity and equality of all peoples as well as individual liberty and guarantying personal emancipation deserves to be called progressive *and the* opposite retrogressive. Human culture is not a static *phenomenon* and therefore there maybe need for me to further explain. Today we live in a duality paradigm as I said earlier, where there are two faces to everything, there is right and wrong, black and white, republicans and democrats, liberals and conservatives as described by some schools of thought. I would however like to see a future multidimensional, dynamic global culture. *An* all encompassing but truly progressive *potpourri* of global ideas, art, philosophy, music dances, folklore *and fashion,* you name it. True human freedom for responsible expression!

Why do I say responsible expression? Because if *it is* not responsible, and in the name of free speech we denigrate fellow humans and promote conflict, then *that expression* becomes irresponsible and retrogressive. Today in America, the mass media is owned by a few giant conglomerates who therefore wield a lot of power by their ability to manipulate what you watch on TV or listen to on the radio, who you vote for, what you buy and so on and so forth without you even realizing it.

In Europe and many developing countries the mass media is in most cases government controlled serving the needs of the ruling elite. Both situations are retrogressive and certainly not multidimensional. There should be a mix of government, individual small holders and some big corporations *in the media industry* to control the hype and also have checks and balances.

As I said earlier also languages need to be preserved and the radio and TV as well as newspapers should be seen to be promoting this language diversity and naturally the other inherent cultural issues. Music on the airwaves, movies, shows and cultural events all carry forward powerful cultural messages and philosophies and need to be promoted multi-dimensionally.

In my opinion all beings and their cultures are born equal: they should live equal and die equal regardless of their net worth. The human self-worth, that sense of human dignity should be viewed *in the same manner*. Only then can true understanding and tolerance be fostered. Only then will we have a true Doctrine of Common Good.

Future Global energy policy: energy consumption is closely linked to human migration, growing urbanization, development and resource depletion. Today we grapple with rural- urban migration. Countries have tried to bring industrialization to rural areas with consequent encroachment on farm land, natural habitats and wasteland followed by inadvertent siltation and environmental destruction, disappearance of forests and extinction of some flora and fauna. Coupled with all this human activity has been increased use of fossil fuels resulting in increased carbon dioxide and carbon monoxide *emissions* and the resultant greenhouse effect and global depletion of the ozone layer, leading to more glaciers melting, desertification, increased flooding and Tsunamis, heat waves and concomitant agricultural disasters. *As global* temperatures continue to rise, this can easily become an uncontrollable spiral.

It would seem that our desire to self improve leads to self destruction. While nuclear power plants do not emit the so called green house gases, their toxic byproducts *scare* the general population. *Governments,* not knowing what to do with nuclear waste, have simply stopped building new power plants. Also disasters like the one at Chernobyl have convinced us that nuclear plants are not that safe.

So what then for the future of global energy production? First, I propose that the current *International Atomic Energy Commission* be restructured into a global energy commission. *That global* body would then promote use of renewable energy sources like solar power and look into new sources of energy. The seas and oceans hold massive amounts of energy. If we can somehow figure out how to create controlled tsunami-like scenarios and use those to generate hydroelectric power, or if we can come up with ways to directly tap electrons from the sea water and channel them to electrical plants we would have boundless amounts of energy. The vast sand deserts and their sand storms can also be used as potential energy sources. Solar energy has not been fully utilized yet. *Clearly* the mars rover, initially thought to have enough energy for three months, has been roving mars now for more than three years with advanced solar panels.

The challenge I see is how to make *that* technology affordable and readily available. But there is hope on the other hand, especially when we look at e-mail and cell-phones. *Those technologies,* which were once clandestine possessions for intelligence people, are now readily available and affordable partly because of the profit incentive on corporations in the electronic industry and the discovery of the microchip. I believe that with the current human and material resources we have, the new global energy commission can spearhead appropriate research and production incentives into long term sustainable and renewable energy sources. Without a clean alternative energy source, mankind would be heading for environmental and self-destruction hence we need to act with urgency.

It is encouraging that countries like Germany have achieved in some cities more than twenty percent energy contributions from solar power clearly illustrating my point that with appropriate policies and incentives humans will find amazing solutions. Every geographical region would, with time, be able to identify the most cost effective yet cleanest energy source in their locality. An appropriate energy policy is paramount to future human development on this planet. To that end it is encouraging to note that there is global consensus for once on the threat to our livelihood posed by the current energy dictum and that humanity is beginning to work towards an ultimate solution. Perhaps our very concept of what true development is needs re-examining.

Global transportation in the future: Today in airline travel and global shipping we see the best level of international cooperation, though still hampered by regional protectionist tendencies and financial limitations imposed by the need for so called hard currency in areas where there would otherwise be well expanded transport networks had it not been for this restriction amongst other problems. With a unitary government system and numerous shipping companies, the key would be to develop an efficient equitable global transport network. Speed, efficiency, availability, punctuality, use of renewable energy sources, will be the *hallmark* of operations. Today each region of the world and sometimes, many countries in one region have different rail systems each with different width and breadth, very compartmentalized and existing within a closed national network, something that will have to change with the adoption of a single international rail system with a single track width and a common approach to safety and all aspects of technical harmonization of the current different national networks. Operationally I think the Japanese bullet train and its operation is perhaps the closest to the beginning of what will become a transcontinental rail system that will evolve and transit long distances, including even under oceans and huge lakes.

The airplane will have to be more adaptable in terms of size, capacity, air time, available services, landing requirements, using renewable energy sources and efficiency. I believe we will see a generation of people who will literary live in the air like today's cruise ships. IATA already exists and only needs to adapt to a unitary currency and changing demands and technologies. The real challenge will be transforming the undeveloped areas of the world into highly accessible productive and *self-sustaining* regions where people achieve their aspirations in all areas. To do this end air transportation will serve as the tool opening up and creating linkages. A lot of these regions have a lot of resources but have been frustrated by currency limitations, poor market access, unfavorable trade conditions, low technological growth and falling further behind in development and thus becoming less and less competitive on a global scale. I have already covered some of the ways that I thing we can remove some of these global distortions in the future.

Talking about transportation without including practical road and telecommunication networks would not be complete. Based on technological trends I believe wireless is going to dominate telecommunication in the future and *revolutionize* communication on a grand scale, in a more cost-effective *but* less capital intensive manner. The current expensive transoceanic underwater and underground fiber optic and cable networks will be *things* of the past. The home telephone and fax as we know them today will be forgotten and replaced completely by wireless type networks. I also believe that we will continue to see newer and better forms of technologies as all regions of the world gain research and productive capacity and competition between different producers spur more efficiency and cost saving.

To conclude, the current selfish tendencies of the powerful few have in effect dragged all of us down. These tendencies need to be discarded to allow for the emergence of a new order aiming for the maximal utilization of both material and human resources in an environmentally self sustaining manner. The order will be guided by the Doctrine of Common Good, under the auspices of a global government with a single currency, police force, judiciary, and parliament. Together with the various arms of its global government, they will all work to preserve human dignity, in line with the universal declaration of human rights.

References:

1: IPCC 3 Climate Change 2007: climate change impacts, adaptation and vulnerability

2: Power station harnesses sun's rays. By David Shukman Science correspondent BBC News Seville May 2 2007

3: Carter And The Rhodesian Problem. International Social Science Review, Fall- Winter 2000 by Paul E. Masters.

4: The Tar Baby Option: American Policy toward Southern Rhodesia. By Lake, Anthony 1976 chapter 7 Irony in Chrome. The Consequences of the Byrd Amendment.

5: International Telecommunications satellites Organization (ITSO) 31st assembly of Parties 20-23 March 2007 Treaty Agreement

6: The International Telecommunications Union (ITU) Encyclopedia of the Nations : United Nations related agencies.

7: World Health Organization (WHO) Encyclopedia of the nations: United Nations related agencies.

8: International Court of Justice (ICJ): www.un.org.law

9: Zimbabwe: Human Rights Report- US Shoots own feet. Opinion The Herald May 2 2007. Caesar Zvayi

10: Results of the Rome conference for an International Criminal Court. The American Society of International Law

11: Reasonable Doubt The case against the Proposed International Criminal Court. By Gary T. Dempsey July 16 1998 Cato Institute Policy analysis No 311

12: The Crimes within the jurisdiction of the international criminal court. European Journal of crime, criminal law and criminal justice. Vol 6/4 1998 377-399 Lyal S. Sunga

13: US Opposition to the International criminal court :Global policies; general documents, analysis and articles on the ICC. www.global. org/intljustice/icc/usindex.htm

14: North, D. Institutions, institutional change and Economic Performance. 1990 Cambridge University Press Cambridge

15: International justice and the international criminal court: between sovereignty and the rule of law. Bruce Broomhall: Oxford: Oxford University Press ISBN 019927424x

16: The International criminal court: The making of the Rome statute. The Hague: Kluwer Law International 1999 ISBN 90-411-1212-x

17: Johannes Morsink, The Universal Declaration of Human Rights: origins, drafting and intent. Philadelphia: University of Pennsylvania Press, 1999.

18: Universal declaration of Human Rights: Wikipedia free encyclopedia

19: Universal human Rights and Human Rights in Islam: David Littman journal Midstream New York Feb/Mar 1999

20: The Cairo Declaration on Human Rights in Islam (CDHRI). The Organization of the Islamic Conference (OIC) August 5 1990

21: Kazemi Farouh "Perspectives on Islam and Civil Society" in

Islamic Political Ethics: civil Society, Pluralism and Conflict, Sohail H. Hashmi, ed. Princeton University Press, 2002 ISBN 0-691-11310-6

22: Anup Shah Arms Trade- a major cause of suffering . Landmines-www.Global issues.org/ArmsTrade/ Landmines.asp July 20 1998 updated Sept 18 2006

23: Chris Hedley: FAO code of conduct for responsible fisheries; internet guide to International fisheries Law www.oceanlaw.net/texts/faocode.htm

24: United Nations Charter: www.UN.org/aboutun/charter

25: United Nations: Wikipedia free encyclopedia

en.wikipedia.org/wiki/United-Nations

26: United Nations General Assembly: Encyclopedia of the Nations

27: 2005 World Summit on Millenium Development Goals and Reform of the United Nations: www.un.org/about mdgs

28: United Nations System:en.wikipedia.org/wiki/united_nations_system

29: History of The United Nations- www.UN.org/aboutun/unhistory

30: International Criminal Police Organization (Interpol): Interpol's five priority crime areas www.interpol.int/default.asp

31: Assad Kotaite "Aviation Regulation: New Millenium-New Direction" 56th IATA annual General Meeting, Sydney 5 June 2000 www.icao.int/icao/en/pres/pres_sydney.htm

32: New EU measures to revitalise freight. International railway

Journal, march 2002

33: Ralph Mathekga. South Africa: Bold Leadership Vital As UN Fails Its Task April26 2007 Business Day Opinion April 26 2007

34: Walden Bello. On Secretary General Annan's Vision of Freedom from Fear. (Monitoring Policy making at the United Nations.) Focus on the Global South Seminar on "In larger Freedom" Makati Phillipines September 6 2005.www.globalpolicy. org/reform/intro/0906visionhtm

35: US admits Afghan civilians killed. BBC News Last update May 11 2007 news.bbc.co.uk/2/hi/south_asia/6647005.stm

36: US Marine shot unarmed Iraqis. BBC News Last updated May 11 2007 news.bbc.co.uk/2/hi/middle_east/6641843.stm

37: Bosnia war dead figure announced. BBC NEWS Last updated June 21 2007 news.bbc.co.uk/2/hi/Europe/6228152.stm

38: The role and mandate of the International Labor organization: encyclopedia of the Nations; United nations related agencies ILO

39: The Report of the World Commission on the Social Dimensions of Globalization. ILO www.ilo.org/public/english/fairglobalization/ report/index.htm

40: Worlds in collision: Terror and the future of Global Order. Ken Booth and Tim Dunne (Palgrave/MacMillan)

41: "Legal issues in The Nicaragua" Appraisal of the ICJ decision Nicaragua versus USA. Morrison, Fred L American Journal of International Law 81 Jan 1987   160-166

ISBN 142516747-0